MY GREAT OUTDOORS BOOK

The kids' guide to being outside

This edition published in the US in 2018 by

Ivy Kids

An imprint of The Quarto Group

The Old Brewery

6 Blundell Street

London N7 9BH

United Kingdom

www.QuartoKnows.com

First published in the UK as *Outdoor Wonderland* in 2014 by Ivy Kids

A CIP record of this book is available from the Library of Congress

ISBN: 978-1-78240-605-1

This book was conceived, designed & produced by

Ivy Kids

58 West Street, Brighton BN1 2RA, United Kingdom

CREATIVE DIRECTOR Peter Bridgewater

MANAGING EDITOR Hazel Songhurst

COMMISSIONING EDITOR Georgia Amson-Bradshaw

PROJECT EDITOR Dereen Taylor

ART DIRECTOR Kim Hankinson

DESIGNERS Clare Barber and Kevin Knight

ILLUSTRATOR Alice Lickens

Printed in China

1 3 5 7 9 10 8 6 4 2

Competent adult supervision is required for many of the activities
in this book. All safety and supervision advice given should be fully
adhered to. Every effort has been made to ensure that all information
in this book is accurate. Neither the publisher nor the author can be
held responsible for any injury, loss or other damages which may
result from the use of information in this book.

MY GREAT OUTDOORS BOOK

The kids' guide to being outside

JOSIE JEFFERY

ILLUSTRATED BY

ALICE LICKENS

IVY KIDS

Contents

About This Book

Are you always being told to go outside and play, but don't know what to do once you get there? Well, help is here! This book is packed with exciting activities and adventures, inspiring all the ideas you need to make the most of the amazing outdoor wonderland at your doorstep.

The book is divided into sections with fun activity ideas for all kinds of weather, so rain won't keep you from playing any more! There are also different sections with activities for wherever you are—whether in the park, a yard, the woods, near water, on the street—and even after darkness falls.

So whatever the weather, and whether you're in a sleepy town, the urban jungle, at the shore, or deep in the country, this book has all you need to keep your friends, family, and YOU busy all through the day and even after dark!

With so many awesome activities, you'll never be bored again—just grab this book and explore the outdoor wonderland!

What will you do today?

You could head into the woods and build a den, or design a bug hotel for your outdoor space. Why not organize a Park Olympics day, an urban animal safari, or a street party? If you're feeling artistic, you could create cloud art, rain paintings, or mossy woodland sculptures. If you're in the mood for learning a new skill, try skipping the perfect stone, playing the grass trumpet, or learning how to become a wildlife photographer. And if you're still looking for something to do after sunset, you could enjoy a star-gazing session or watch an enchanting performance at the moth theater.

Helper Bug

When Helper Bug appears, you need an adult to give you assistance. This will ensure the best results!

Danger Bug

When Danger Bug appears, be extra careful! An adult MUST supervise the activity to keep you safe.

It's time to get yourself outside & have some FUN!

Grow It, Eat It!

If you've ever picked your own strawberries, you know how much better they taste than strawberries bought at the store. So just imagine how stupendously scrumptious strawberries that you've actually grown yourself will taste!

Berry backpack

You can grow your strawberries in special grow-bags or in pots… or you could try something a bit different, and plant them in an old backpack instead!

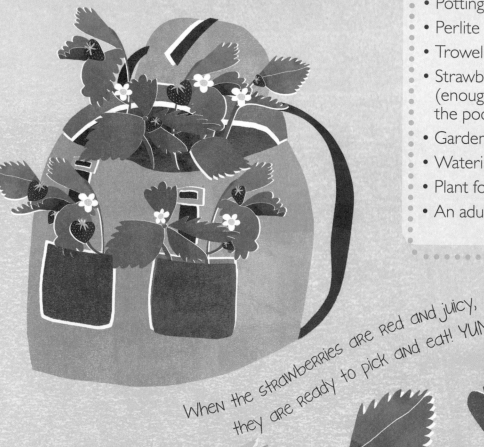

When the strawberries are red and juicy, they are ready to pick and eat! YUM, YUM!

Birds beware!

To make sure that birds don't eat all your strawberries before you do, you can make an excellent bird guard using string, old CDs and tinfoil. Thread a CD onto the string, then cover the string either side of it with a twist of tinfoil about 2 inches long. Alternate the CDs and the foil until the string is full. Hang your bird guard above your strawberry plants by tying it between two garden canes. Ta da!

1 Ask an adult to make small holes in the base of the backpack and at the bottom of the pockets using a screwdriver. Place the backpack in a sunny spot, out of the wind.

2 Put a layer of pebbles or stones in the base and in the pockets for drainage. Then cover with potting soil mixed with a handful of perlite. The perlite helps the potting soil to stay moist.

3 Dig holes in the potting soil with your trowel and drop the plants in, then cover the roots with soil. Carefully pat down the soil around the plants, and water.

4 Cover loosely with netting to keep birds from munching on the berries. Water daily and, when white flowers appear, feed once a week. These flowers will eventually turn into fruits.

Bee Friendly!

Bees are super important when it comes to helping things grow—in fact, we'd be in big trouble without them. You can get to know your busy little visitors better, and help them out, by making your yard or garden a bee-friendly haven.

Busy bee survey

To find out how many bees buzz through your yard or garden each day you need paper and colored pens, and an area where some bee-friendly flowering plants grow.

Down the side of your paper, write the information you want to survey. You could count the different types of bees that visit and which plants they like the most. Across the top, note the times when you will be surveying. Stay for ten minutes each time and count how many bees come buzzing by...

Tip Try not to be too noisy or move too suddenly, or you will disturb the bees!

NUMBER OF VISITS

Types of bee	8am	12pm
Honeybee		
Bumblebee		
Carpenter bee		

Go green
If you really want to get your garden buzzing, try planting scented, open-flowered plants such as alliums, daisies, lavender, oriental poppies, and snapdragons.

BUZZ

BUZZ

4pm	7pm	Plants visited

Bees at work
Bees do a really important job in your yard. As they buzz around your plants, they pass pollen from one flower to another. This is called "pollination," which is how many flowering plants make seeds that will grow into new plants. About one-third of everything we eat depends on pollination by bees!

LAVENDER

SNAPDRAGON

Bee fact
There are about 20,000 different species of bees in the world!

Ready, Set, GROW!

Are you a green-fingered gardening wizard? Growing plants may seem like magic, especially when bulbs sprout up months after you planted them, but really it's super-easy!

Amazing bulb spiral

Many different types of flowers grow from bulbs, including hyacinths, daffodils, tulips, and bluebells. Bulbs "sleep" underground until the time is right for them to grow and to flower. You can't see them until they sprout, so it's fun to plant "invisible" patterns during fall, that will magically appear in the spring.

One great project you can do over a few days is to plant a flower spiral that you can walk around. The steps show you how to make a spiral around 6.5 feet wide.

1 Lay out one piece of rope in a spiral. Leave about 20 inches between each coil.

2 Lay out the second rope next to the first, so they are about 10 inches apart.

3 Dig a trench between the ropes. It should be 8 inches wide and twice the depth of your bulbs. Place the turf you remove to the side.

4 Lay your bulbs in the trench a few inches apart. Make sure the roots are facing downward.

5 Fill in the trench and replace the turf, then lightly press it down with your feet.

6 When you have planted the bulbs all the way along your spiral, water it well. Then just wait for the flowers to appear in spring!

Tip In a big yard, you can increase the scale of your spiral by doubling the length of rope and the number of bulbs.

Flower Power

Flowers only last a few days once you've picked them, but there is a simple way to make them last much longer—flower pressing. It will keep your love of nature blooming!

Press to impress!

The simplest way to press flowers is between the pages of a heavy book. Remember to protect the book's pages from staining by placing the flower between two sheets of tissue first.

Follow the tips shown on the petals below, and you'll be well on your way to pressing success.

Choose flowers with simple shapes

Try just pressing petals

Make sure flowers are dry

Leave for two weeks

Lay leaves out flat

Always ask before you pick

Pick differently shaped flowers

Press flowers soon after picking

Sparkling sun catcher

Once your pressed flowers are ready, you can make a sparkling sun catcher to show them off.

1 Place your pressed flowers onto the flat side of one of the acrylic blocks, choosing one corner as the "top" of your picture.

2 Using the toothpick, carefully stick the flowers in place with tiny dots of glue. Allow the glue to dry.

3 Cut four strips of tape slightly longer than the sides of the blocks. Put the second block on top of the flowers and wrap tape around the bottom two sides to hold the blocks together. Make sure the tape is straight.

4 Bend the picture wire to make a loop at the top, leaving two long ends at the bottom pointing out.

5 Position the loop at the top corner and place the wire ends along the sides. Neatly tape over these ends as you wrap tape around the top two sides of the layered blocks.

6 Trim the tape at the corners and tie a ribbon onto the loop. Then hang your sun catcher in the window and watch it sparkle!

At The Bug Hotel

Get insects and other animals to check in to their own luxury hotel by building a cozy habitat for them to shelter in over the winter. This recycled shelter will cost nothing to make… but it will be worth a million to your guests!

The big build

✳ Start off by building the frame. Place crates or pallets on top of each other, or use old planks of wood layered on top of bricks. Turn the gaps into guest rooms by putting in paper tubes, pebbles, potted plants, upside-down flower pots, logs, bricks, and tiles.

✳ Decorate each "room" with dry leaves, straw, twigs, moss, feathers, and bark—anything that will keep your guests sheltered and warm.

Frogs and toads will hop under bricks and tiles.

Bees and other insects love bedding down in old potted plants.

Be an insect expert

Entomologists are insect experts. You can be an entomologist, too, by keeping a close eye on one type of insect that visits your hotel. Do they check in alone, or with other guests? Do they build a nest or bed down in the comfortable surroundings? By the end of their stay, you will know much more about your chosen insect and their habits.

Tip This is a great group activity, so ask friends and family to choose a "room" to decorate!

Dawn and Dusk

What's the difference between day and night? Is it just the amount of light? Check out the wildlife in your yard at each end of the day, and you'll find there's much more to it than that…

What is dawn?

Dawn is the first appearance of light before sunrise, early in the morning.

Birdsong

You may have heard of bird-watching, but have you heard of bird-listening? It's when you close your eyes and really listen to the sounds that birds make.

At dawn, birds sing more loudly than they do at other times of the day, and the air is often cool and still, making the sounds easier to hear. This is called the "dawn chorus", and it is best heard during spring. Different birds have different calls and songs—some even sound like they are speaking! Listen carefully to what the birds are saying in your yard. It may surprise you!

GET RECORDING

Try recording the sounds made by wildlife in your yard at dawn and at dusk and compare your findings.

• When is it noisiest?

• Which is the noisiest animal at dawn, and at dusk?

• What kind of wildlife is most active at dawn— birds or other types of animals?

What is dusk?

Dusk is the period at the end of the day between light and darkness.

Getting dark

In many places, it takes about 30 minutes to get dark after the sun has set, but this varies depending on where you are. You can find out how long it takes where you live by timing from the moment the sun sets until total darkness. Once darkness has fallen, find a quiet spot and see what nocturnal visitors to your yard you can see—or hear.

Bat fact

Bats emerge from their daytime roosts at dusk. They have poor eyesight and use echolocation—this means they send out high-pitched beeps and listen for changes in the echoes that bounce back at them. This allows them to figure out which direction to go in and where to find their food.

GET EXPERIMENTING

Ask friends and family around the country, or even the world, to join in an experiment to see if it takes the same length of time to get dark in different places. There's a useful website on page 76 that tells you what time the sun will set in your neighborhood.

The Sun Goes Down

Just because it's getting dark doesn't mean it's time to go indoors. You can still make the most of the amazing outdoors as darkness falls!

Sunset silhouette painting

There's only one way to describe a spectacular, fiery sky at sunset—wow! Sunset happens daily as the sun disappears below the horizon, but sometimes, when the conditions are right, it creates stunning, dramatic colors in the sky. Here's one way of capturing that perfect moment of color and natural beauty.

YOU WILL NEED

- A beautiful sunset to inspire you
- White paper
- Paints, pastels, or colored chalks
- Paintbrush
- Easel or board

1 Pick a building or tree that stands out against the sky. As the light dims, the object will become darker, until it is a silhouette. It is this contrast between the black outline and the colorful sky that will make your picture dramatic.

2 Place your piece of paper on an easel or board, and paint your sunset background using red, pink and orange colors. Allow to dry.

3 Using black paint, carefully paint the outline of the silhouette over the colorful background, trying to keep it really sharp, then fill it in.

Flash tag

How about a game of Tag with a fun nighttime twist? All you need is a group of at least three friends with flashlights and a safe, dark space to play in.

The more friends playing and the more places there are to hide, the better the game will be.

It's all about stealth and tactics rather than simply outrunning the person who is "it."

Tip Make sure you flash your light on and off super fast, so that you don't get noticed!

1 Everyone has one minute to run off in different directions with their flashlights (which are turned off).

2 Taking care not to be seen, each player goes on a hunt for their friends.

3 If someone manages to sneak up and shine their flashlight on another player, then that player is out!

Repeat step 3 until only one stealthy tagger is left— and they are the winner of the game!

Twinkle, Twinkle...

Look up on a clear, cloud-free night… the sky is alive with twinkling stars! Each one is trillions of miles away. The light coming from them has taken many years to reach us.

Connect the star dots

If you know what you are looking for, you can see star groups, called constellations. Ask an adult to help you find star maps and star-gazing advice on the Internet.

Leo

Sirius

Great Dog

Orion

The constellation of Leo represents a lion. The part that looks like a backward question mark is the lion's head. Leo can be seen most clearly during the months of March, April, and May.

The Great Dog constellation is easy to recognize as it contains the brightest star in the entire night sky—Sirius. The Great Dog is most clearly visible during January, February, and March.

Orion is one of the easiest constellations to find. It has an hourglass shape, with a 3-star band, Orion's Belt, in the middle. It is most clearly visible during December, January, and February.

Be a star expert

An astronomer is a scientist who studies moons, planets, and stars—and you can be one tonight! Check out the moon and, using the chart here, figure out where it is in its monthly cycle. Is it nearer to the full moon (complete moon visible) or the new moon (no moon visible)? See if you can track the moon for a month, and each night draw what you see or take a photograph to record your very own moon cycle!

Star struck There is one star you can always see during the day—the sun! It is the star at the center of our solar system.

Meteor showers

If you watch the sky from a dark location, you may see dazzling streaks of light from meteors, or "shooting stars." These are pieces of space debris that burn up when they get close to the earth. Several times a year, comets pass close to the earth, leaving a stream of debris that make a stunning meteor shower.

The Secret Garden

Shh… it's bedtime… but not for everyone! Outside is a whole new place at night, with nocturnal creatures getting out of their beds just as you are getting ready for yours.

A moth theater

Moths have beautiful wings like butterflies, but most only come out at night. You've probably seen them fluttering around street lights—they are attracted to bright lights. You can use this behavior to get them to put on a fabulous show just for you!

YOU WILL NEED

- A large white sheet and permission to paint on it
- Colored paints
- Clothesline and clothespins to hang up your sheet
- Heavy stones to weigh down the bottom of the sheet
- A bright white light (such as a bright flashlight)
- A comfortable chair—and some popcorn

1 First, paint stage curtains onto your sheet. Add a row of audience members along the bottom, if you like. Make sure you leave a large white space in the middle of the sheet.

2 Hang the sheet from a clothesline, or tape it to a wall. Weigh down the bottom with stones so that it doesn't flap around too much.

3 Position the bright light. Either place a lamp in front of the sheet, or hang a flashlight from the clothesline.

4 Turn on the light when it begins to get dark. Set your chair in front of the sheet, and watch as moths begin to fly in. They will flutter and dance around the light, and will land on the sheet too, so you can get a close-up look.

5 Munch your popcorn and enjoy the show!

Moth fact

The scientific name for butterflies and moths is "Lepidoptera," which means "scaly winged." This is because the pretty patterns on their wings are made up of thousands of tiny overlapping scales. There are more than 250,000 species of moth, and they come in all different colors, shapes, and sizes.

Park Life

It's really easy to spend a terrific day at the park. With the great ideas in this section, you won't even think about heading for the swings and slides!

Climb a tree

Make sure an adult is nearby! Find a tree with strong, large branches that can support your weight. To stay safe, keep three of your limbs on the tree at all times. Look for holes to hook into with your hands and feet, and smaller branches that you can use as footholds. Take it slowly and enjoy the view.

Grass trumpets

Pick a thin, flat blade of grass, from a nice clean spot. Press your thumbs together side-to-side, with the grass sandwiched between them. Place your lips against your thumbs and slowly blow through the gap —you'll hear a surprisingly loud sound!

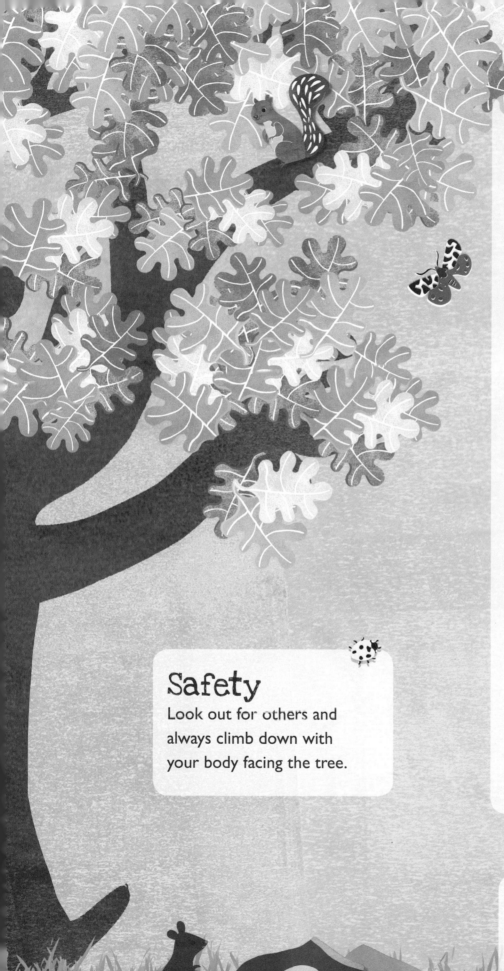

Park survival basics

Before you head for the park, make sure you have plenty of picnic supplies, and don't forget the all-important picnic blanket—perfect for canopy making, as well as for sitting on!

At the park, scout out the best terrain for your base camp. On a hot day, a shady spot under a tree is best. You can drape your blanket on low branches to make your canopy.

Water will stay cooler for longer "buried" in the soil. Just make sure the bottle is well sealed!

Safety
Look out for others and always climb down with your body facing the tree.

Go green
Don't forget to put litter in a trashcan after your picnic.

On Your Mark

The great thing about the park is that there's so much space for everyone to run around—it's the perfect place to stage your very own Park Olympics. The more people that compete, the better! You could try these events…

Walking Wardrobe

YOU WILL NEED

- Two sets of clothing and accessories (things you might need at the park—two pairs of sunglasses, two sweatshirts, etc.)
- Two teams

� Lay out the sets of clothes in two parallel lines, with about three feet between each item. The first players from each team race to put on and then take off each item as quickly as they can. They then run back and tag the next player to go.

My Shoe Flew!

YOU WILL NEED

- A clear, open space
- A shoe to throw
- A group of throwers, each with a pebble or popsicle stick to use as a marker

� Take it in turns to see who can throw the shoe the farthest.

� Each player should mark their landing spot with a marker.

� Use clothing to form circles, then land a shoe inside a circle to win extra kudos!

Capture the Flag

YOU WILL NEED

- A large area with plenty of hiding places
- Two flags—hats or water bottles will also work
- Two teams

✳ The playing area is divided into three—one territory belonging to each team, and a neutral space (belonging to neither) in the middle. Each territory has a small "jail" section.

✳ Each team secretly hides their flag in their territory. Players must find and grab the opposing team's flag without getting caught on enemy territory.

✳ If a player finds an enemy team member on their team's territory, they may take them to jail. Players can only be freed from jail when a member of their own team touches them.

✳ The winning team is the one who captures the other team's flag and brings it back to their own territory.

Red Rover

YOU WILL NEED

- Two teams of at least five players each
- Two team captains

✳ The teams form two parallel lines opposite each other. Each team joins hands to create a chain.

✳ The captain of Team A chooses a player from Team B and invites them to play by calling, "Red Rover, Red Rover, let (choose a player) come over!"

✳ The chosen player then runs at the opposing team and tries to break through their chain.

✳ If the player fails, they join that chain, and the Team A captain chooses another player to take a turn.

✳ If the player succeeds, they go back to Team B, and choose a player from Team A to take a turn breaking their chain.

✳ The game ends when one team has all but one of the players in their chain.

Wild Photography

A great way to really see the park and all the creatures that live in it is to get behind a camera. It is guaranteed to make you view your surroundings in a new way. So get ready to zoom in on nature!

Picture this!

There's so much to see in the park—trees, flowers, birds, and other animals. With the tips below and a bit of practice, you'll be photographing them all like a pro in no time!

Up close
Use the zoom feature to get in close and capture every amazing detail.

Keep shooting
Take lots of shots to make sure you get that one perfect image.

Get an angle on it
Take pictures from unusual angles and viewpoints.

Focus
Place your camera on a steady surface to keep your images sharp.

PHOTO FUN

When you get home, remember to download or print your photos. You could create an on-screen collage, or keep them in an album. Print out an extra set and use your photos to play some cool games, like the ones described on the next page.

Zoom!

If you've taken some mega-zoomed-in shots, you can test your friends' knowledge of nature by seeing if they can recognize what you photographed!

Snap!

Cut your pictures in half, shuffle them and split them into two packs. Use them to play a wild game of Snap!

Pairs

Halved pictures are also perfect for a game of pairs. Mix them up and spread them out, face-down. Take turns trying to flip over two matching halves.

Be a wildlife photographer

A wildlife photographer travels the world taking pictures of wild animals in their natural habitats. And you can be one too! Patience is essential… and you must keep quiet and still. You need to sneak up on the animal you want to photograph, or sit very still and wait for it to come to you. If the animal sees or hears you, it will run away and you will lose your shot!

Nature Watcher

The woods are full of animals and plant life, and even wild food! So keep your eyes peeled and see what you can find…

Get tracking!

Have you ever been at the beach and seen footprints in the sand? Maybe you followed them to find out where they went—this is called "tracking."

You can't always see animals in the wild, but you can find out a lot from what they leave behind. By looking at their footprints, a sharp-eyed tracker can tell what kind of animal passed by, and where it was going. The best place to look for animal tracks is on soft ground, such as mud, snow, or sand.

Bird tracks normally show three toes pointing forward, and one back.

FOX

If you see a paw print with little dots at the front, it is an animal that can't pull in its claws, like a dog or a fox.

DEER

A print with two "toes" is an animal with cloven hooves, such as a deer.

CAT

Cats can pull in their claws, so their paw prints won't have dots in front of the toes.

Be a plant expert

A botanist is a plant expert, and some botanists explore the world looking for new and exotic plants. New plants are given names based on their color, characteristics, who found them, and so on. This naming system was invented way back in 1735 by a Swedish scientist called Carl Linnaeus. This same stystem is still used by botanists today.

You can be a botanist, too! Find a flower in the woods and give it a name. For example, if it's yellow, has four petals, and smells like vanilla, call it "Yellowvanilla fourpetalosa."

Yellowvanilla fourpetalosa

Safety

Never eat unidentified berries as they may be poisonous. Always check with an adult.

Foraging for treats

Berries are a natural, tasty treat. They grow in brambles and hedges in the fall. Watch out for scratchy thorns when you pick them, though. And remember, leave some behind for other people—and birds and wildlife—to enjoy!

Den Building

If you're playing in the woods, you've just got to build a den! There are plenty of different ways to make an amazing den, and this cool camouflaged hideout is just one of them.

Construction tips

For the framework, you'll need to find two trees that are growing 10 or 12 feet apart, two large Y-shaped branches, and a long branch to be the cross-pole.

1 Prop the Y-shaped branches against the two trunks and then place the long cross-pole between the two Y-shaped branches.

2 Balance the branches at an angle against each side of the cross-pole to make the walls of your den. Don't forget to leave an entrance!

3 Use moss, mud, and leaves to camouflage your den. This will also help to rainproof it.

4 A bed of dry leaves or cut hay makes a great carpet inside your den.

5 After all your hard work, you're ready to enjoy hot chocolate and marshmallows!

Take a trunk...

Did you know you can figure out the age of a cut-down tree by looking at its trunk? Just count the number of rings—there is one ring for each year of a tree's life. Can you figure out how old this tree was before it was cut down? There are a lot of rings to count!

You could try a teepee-style den, too!

Go green

Be kind to nature and use building materials that are already on the ground, rather than breaking branches and twigs off plants and trees.

Eco Art

Great works of art don't have to be made on a piece of paper. Land art uses the natural materials around us—such as moss, twigs, branches, leaves, stones, and rocks—to make awesome art, and anyone can do it, anywhere!

I love hearts and spirals

Collect piles of woodland treasures such as small stones, pine cones, horse chestnuts, or leaves. Clear a space and then use your treasure to create gorgeous geometric shapes.

Marvelous moss monster

Create an awesome moss monster using a mossy log for the body, and twigs and branches for the arms. What could you use for your monster's eyes?

Fall leaf chain

Carefully thread pretty fall leaves together to make a delicate leaf chain. To thread the leaves, make a small slit in the bottom half of a leaf and push the stalk of the second leaf through it. You can make the chain secure by then weaving the stalk back through the leaf, ending with the stalk at the back of the chain. Work from the largest leaf down to the smallest. Hang the chain from a tree to catch the sunlight—and leave it for the next passerby to enjoy!

Go green

Be a respectful land artist by making sure you don't damage any plants when you hunt for your art materials.

Land art fact

There are many talented land artists who use natural materials to create amazing art. One is Robert Smithson, who created the beautiful Spiral Jetty at the Great Salt Lake in Utah. This incredible structure is made out of mud, rocks, and salt crystals, and is over 1,500 feet long and nearly 15 feet wide.

Watch It Blow!

Stand with your eyes closed and feel the wind blowing around you. You might not be able to see the wind, but you can certainly feel it!

Leaf catcher

Play this game on a windy fall day. Keep your eyes on the skies, and when the wind blows, try to catch any falling leaves before they hit the ground. If you are playing with other people, the winner is the person who catches the most!

Roaring dragon windsock

A windsock shows the direction the wind is blowing, and this dragon does it with style!

YOU WILL NEED

- Old, long-sleeved shirt
- Scissors
- 12-inch length of wire
- Needle and thread
- Felt
- Palm-sized, flat, smooth stone
- 3-foot length of string
- An adult helper

1 Cut the shirt sleeve off at the shoulder seam. Bend the wire into a circle, the same size as the top of the sleeve.

2 Ask an adult to help you fold over ¾-inch of fabric to cover the wire, and then stitch the wire in place.

3 Your dragon has a mouth! Cut the felt to create eyes and scales, then sew them on.

4 Take the leftover fabric and cut out a square to make a pocket for the stone.

The stone helps keep the windsock facing into the wind.

5 With the windsock inside out, attach the pocket at the dragon's "chin," by sewing along three sides. Place the stone inside, then sew the fourth side.

6 Turn the windsock right-side out. Cut the string in half and sew the end of each piece to the sides of the dragon's mouth.

7 Tie your windsock to a high branch. Your dragon will show you what direction the wind is blowing!

Musical Airs

Have you ever listened to the amazing sounds the wind makes? It whistles, wails, and howls… You can use the power of the wind to make other noises, too!

YOU WILL NEED

- Metal flatware (with a ridge where the handle joins the blade)
- Long pipe cleaners (one for each piece of flatware)
- Beads
- String
- Scissors
- A small branch on a tree
- An adult helper

Flatware wind chime

Wind chimes are outdoor mobiles. The dangling metal makes jangling noises as the wind knocks the chimes together. You can make this simple wind chime using old metal flatware.

1 Knot the end of a pipe cleaner around the top of the handle of a piece of flatware, leaving a long end of pipe cleaner sticking out.

Jingle shells

Look for seashells and pebbles with holes in them. Thread string through the holes, tying a knot on each side of the hole to secure each pebble and shell. Between the shells and stones, thread some beads and knot in place. Repeat with more pieces of string. Tie the strings to a coat hanger, about one inch apart, and hang them outside, then listen to the shells jingle in the wind!

2 Add a bead to the pipe cleaner, and then wind the pipe cleaner around the handle, adding beads as you go. End with a large bead and knot the pipe cleaner around the flatware to secure it.

3 Repeat steps 1 and 2 with each piece of flatware. Then tie a 12-inch piece of string around the top bead on each piece.

4 Tie each piece of flatware to the branch. Hang them close enough that the wind will knock them together.

Windy Day Play

The wind is great for keeping things moving—kites, boats, leaves—and you! Get on the move with some wild windy-day play.

Wobbly jellyfish kite

You make the jellyfish… and the wind will make it wobble!

YOU WILL NEED

- Large brown paper bag
- Hole punch
- Hole reinforcement labels
- Scissors
- Two five-foot lengths of strong string
- Colored markers
- PVA glue
- Paper streamers or strips of crepe paper

1 Flatten the bag and punch two holes at the top (open) end, about one inch down and one inch in from the corners. Stick hole reinforcement labels on both sides of the four holes.

2 Cut one of the pieces of string in half. Create a handle on each side of the bag by threading the string through the holes, from the outside in, and knotting securely.

4 Decorate the bag body of your jellyfish using colored pens.

5 Glue paper streamers to the lower section of the paper bag to make tentacles.

Leaf-sail boat race

Sailboats need wind to power them…
and so do cute little leaf-sail boats!

These boats are easy to make using a piece of
bark for the boat, a strong twig for the mast,
and a large leaf for the sail. Carefully thread the
twig through the leaf to make a sail, and push
the twig mast into the bark. Find a stream or
large puddle, and your boat is ready to race!

3 Loop one end of the
second piece of string
through both handles and
tie in a knot.

6 Once the glue is
dry… your kite is
ready to fly!

Lean into a gust of wind,
arms out, like a bird.
A really strong wind will
support you very briefly!

Hello, Rain!

When the rain starts, the outdoor fun doesn't have to stop. There are still plenty of great activities to do outside—you can measure the rain, splash in it, even lie down and make art in it!

Rain shadows

If it's starting to rain, don't rush inside… stay and make rain shadows! Pick a safe spot—such as your deck or a path in the park, and lie down when the rain starts. Stay still while the rain wets the ground around you—when you get up, there will be a dry area, which is your rain shadow.

You can make great rain shadows from other objects too, like your bike or scooter. The best shadows are made on stone or tarmac.

Be a weather expert

A meteorologist is an expert who collects information about the weather. You can be one, too, by using your rain catcher (opposite) to measure how much rain is falling when there's a heavy shower. How about when it's just a light shower? Try comparing the amount of rain to the length of time the shower lasted.

Rain catcher

Ever wondered how much rain is really falling?
This rain catcher lets you measure it!

YOU WILL NEED

- A clear plastic water bottle (without a lid)
- Scissors
- Stickers
- Permanent markers
- Clear waterproof varnish
- Brush
- Long wooden spoon
- Ruler
- 2 thick pipe cleaners
- Gravel
- An adult helper

1 Ask an adult to help you cut the top off the bottle, about three-quarters of the way up. You will need the top for step 5.

2 Decorate the bottle using stickers and markers, then ask an adult to cover it with a layer of varnish.

3 Lay the spoon next to the ruler. Starting ¼-inch up, mark lines at ¼-inch intervals along the handle with a permanent marker.

4 Draw a face on the front of the spoon. Make a shirt by winding a pipe cleaner around the neck of the spoon. Use another pipe cleaner to make arms.

5 Fill the bottom of the bottle with gravel, and fit the upside-down top of the bottle inside the decorated bottle.

6 Place your rain catcher in an open spot in your yard or garden. After a rain shower, dip your rain man measure in to see how much rain has fallen!

Rain Painting

A rainy day doesn't have to be a washout—it can be a great opportunity to get creative, and you can even use the rain water in your art!

Beat it!

Hapa Zome is the Japanese art of beating leaves and flowers to pound their natural colors into cloth. The more moisture there is in the leaves and flowers, the better the results will be—petals picked just after a rain shower are perfect!

YOU WILL NEED

- Cotton cloth rectangle
- A selection of moist leaves and flowers
- Mallet or large, smooth stone
- Picture frame to fit the size of the cloth
- Smooth surface to work on
- An adult helper

1 Fold the cloth in half and make a crease line. Open up the cloth and use the leaves and flowers to make a design on just the right-hand side of the crease.

2 Fold the left side of the cloth over to cover the design. Ask an adult to help you gently pound the cloth with a mallet or stone.

3 Carefully open up the cloth to reveal your image. You can then frame it to create a special gift.

Raindrop art

Mud, food coloring, and charcoal work just as well as paint when it comes to making rain pictures. Just make blobs on a large piece of paper and leave it outside in the rain. Watch from a window to see how the rain transforms the blobs. Bring your picture in when you like the way it looks and lay it down flat to dry.

Tracing and racing

When sitting inside on a cold day, have you ever noticed the layer of water droplets—called condensation—on the inside of the window? You can use your finger to trace a picture in this moisture. Then if you put a piece of colored paper over the traced picture, the paper picks up the wet areas and the picture you traced with your finger stays dry. Magic!

Raindrop races

Have a raindrop race with a friend. Both choose a water droplet at the top of a window, and see which one reaches the bottom first!

Splish, Splash!

Don't stay indoors listening to the sound of the rain…
Go outside with friends and put together a raindrop
orchestra. With pots and pans and sticks and spoons,
you'll soon be making more noise than the rain!

Set the stage

If you know there's a heavy
downpour due, place
different containers
outside, ready to catch the
rain. Mix it up by using
plastic and metal pots in
a range of different sizes.

Sounds like…

Huge containers and
tiny containers filled with
water make different
sounds. Try adding or
reducing the amount of
water in a pot to change
the sound it makes.

Plopping
Catching drops on
upside-down containers

Bashing
Hitting containers with
sticks and spoons

Plunking
Throwing pebbles or
coins into containers

Go green

Don't waste the rainwater you have collected—put it to good use by storing it to water thirsty plants on a dry day. (Or you could use it to fill the water bombs on page 56!)

Splashing
Jumping in a puddle could be the sound to end your tune!

Whooshing
Tipping water between containers

Sloshing
Stirring water around in containers

Sun Time

People have used sundials to tell the time for thousands of years. Building your own super-cool sundial is a fun project for the whole family to work on together in the sunshine.

Super sundial

A sundial uses the position of the sun in the sky to show the time. It has a face and a dial hand that casts a shadow showing how the position of the sun changes from hour to hour.

Plant pots mark the hours 1 to 12.

YOU WILL NEED

- Chalk
- Tape measure
- One 3-foot bamboo cane
- One 8-inch terracotta pot (empty)
- Gravel
- Chalk/paints
- Four 10-inch terracotta pots (filled with plants)
- Eight 4-inch terracotta pots (empty)
- An adult helper

1 Choose your spot—a sunny deck is perfect. Ask an adult to help you chalk out a 4-foot square base. Then carefully chalk a circle inside the base that touches all the sides of the square.

2 To make the dial, stick the bamboo cane in the 8-inch pot and pack gravel around it to hold it upright. Then place the pot in the center of the square base.

3 Using chalk or paint, mark the four large plant pots with the quarter hours of a clock (12, 3, 6, 9).

4 Turn the eight smallest pots upside down and mark them with the remaining hours (1, 2, 4, 5, 7, 8, 10, 11).

5 Each hour, on the hour, check the position of the shadow cast by the cane, and make sure that the pot for that time is in the correct place (under the shadow).

The shadow from the bamboo cane shows the time!

For each of the quarter hours, use a colorful plant.

Tip The accuracy of a sundial changes through the seasons, so you'll need to check your sundial every few weeks and tweak the position of the hour markers to make sure it stays on time.

Cloud watching

Got your head in the clouds? That's not so bad—they are pretty amazing! Clouds are made of tiny droplets of water, and they come in all shapes and sizes.

3-D cloud portraits

Beautiful clouds have inspired artists throughout history. But painting a flat picture of clouds is boring —painting a 3-D picture is much more impressive! Mix one cup of shaving cream with one cup of white glue in a bowl to make thick, fluffy "paint." Dab this onto paper and shape with a spoon to make 3-D clouds that stay puffy when dry.

YOU WILL NEED

- Shaving cream
- White glue
- Colored paper
- A spoon

Tip Add colored paint or food coloring to your shaving cream and glue mixture to make pink and yellow sunset clouds. Pretty!

Be a cloud expert

A nepholographer studies and photographs clouds. If you have a camera, you can be one, too! Find a cloud you like, take a photograph, and print it out. What shape can you see in your cloud? An animal, a person, or a pattern? Sketch in the outline of the shape and then hang it on your wall or send it as a card to a friend!

Sun Printing

You'll be surprised by just how powerful the sun's rays can be. They can even print a picture in a couple of hours—with your help, of course!

YOU WILL NEED

- 2 large sheets of cardboard (big enough to cover your T-shirt)
- Scissors
- A new dark-colored cotton T-shirt
- Markers
- Masking tape
- Craft knife
- Clothespins
- An adult helper

Sunshine reverse stencil

Use the sun to help you create an original and totally hot T-shirt design!

1 Cut the cardboard sheets so they are just bigger than your T-shirt. Draw around the your T-shirt on one sheet of cardboard.

2 Tape your T-shirt to the other sheet of cardboard. Make sure the T-shirt is in the same position as for step 1.

3 Take the first sheet of cardboard and draw a sun design onto the center of the T-shirt outline.

4 Ask an adult to carefully cut the design out of the cardboard using the craft knife.

5 Sandwich the two sheets of card together and fasten the edges with clothespins. Lay them in the sun for several days.

Sunshine silhouettes

On a sunny day get busy with some dark-colored construction paper and an interesting selection of small, solid objects. Maybe coins, pebbles, leaves… or anything else with an interesting shape!

Arrange the objects into a design on the paper, then place in full sunlight—outdoors or on a windowsill—and leave for at least an hour. When the paper has faded, remove the objects to reveal a fab sunshine silhouette. The longer you leave your design sunbathing, the better the result will be!

6 Open up the card… and see the sunshine on your T-shirt!

Safety The sun's rays are mega-powerful! Always protect your skin while you're outdoors by wearing sun protection. Also, never look directly at the sun.

Water Fight!

You don't need water pistols for a fun water fight! There's an arsenal of water blasters ready and waiting around your home, and you can even make your own water bombs!

For the best water fights...

✳ It can get slippery, so find a large, safe area to play in.

✳ Always ask permission before you turn your yard into a splash arena!

Bombs away!

Making your own water bombs is fun —and throwing them is even better!

WATER FIGHT KIT LIST

Buckets
Essential for holding your water supplies

Sponges
Perfect super-soakers for drenching with one good splat!

Squeeze bottles
For a direct squirt that hits the spot!

1 Fold the paper in half diagonally and unfold. Repeat in the other direction to make an X shape.

2 Turn the paper over and fold in half horizontally, top to bottom. Then repeat, side to side.

3 Turn the paper over so the sides are sloping downward and pinch the paper on either side of one diagonal crease, creating a star shape.

4 Carefully flatten down into one triangle shape.

5 Take the bottom corners on the front side and fold them up to the top in the middle. Repeat on the back to make a square.

6 Fold the side corners in to the middle line. This will create little pockets. Turn over and repeat on back.

7 Fold the flap above each pocket out to the side, then fold it back in half to the center, to make a smaller, triangular flap.

8 This flap should then fit neatly inside the pocket. Repeat on the other sides.

9 Blow in the hole in the bottom to inflate, then fill with water.

Tasty Treats

Sunny days are made for eating outdoors—and cooking outdoors, too. So let's set up the campfire kitchen and get those taste buds zinging!

Orange-pot campfire choccy cake

Nothing beats food cooked on a campfire! Next time you're having a campfire cookout try this delicious dessert—gooey chocolate brownie cakes baked inside oranges.

1 Ask an adult to slice the tops off the oranges and then scoop out the flesh with a large spoon.

2 Prepare the brownie cake mix according to the package directions.

Safety

Campfire cooking is fun but can be dangerous! Make sure an adult is supervising at all times.

Sun-dried apple rings

You'll need some peeled, cored apples, sliced into rings about one-quarter inch thick—ask an adult to help you with this. Lay the rings on a mesh tray, and place the tray in a sunny spot raised up on a couple of bricks, so that air can circulate. Cover the fruit with a dish towel to protect it from bugs and birds. Leave it to dry it for several days, turning the rings twice a day and bringing them in at night. Check to see if the fruit is ready by tearing a ring in half—it should feel rubbery. Then eat and enjoy!

3 Fill each orange "pot" with brownie batter, leaving one inch at the top.

4 Add the orange "lids" and tightly wrap each orange in at least two layers of tinfoil.

5 Ask an adult to put them in the campfire embers for around 40 minutes, turning them every so often.

6 Carefully unwrap... and dig in!

Tip Use the flesh from the oranges to flavor the brownie cake mix!

I Spy...

The beach is the perfect place to see weird and wonderful wildlife. And if you paddle in a rock pool when the tide's out, who knows what you may find?

Bird clues

You may see birds at the beach that are different from the ones you see in your yard. Some detective work can help you identify them. Draw or photograph each bird and write down their size and the color of their feathers, feet, and beak. Hunt around for physical clues like feathers and tracks in the sand. Back at home, research your bird online or in a bird-watching book.

Orangey Beak

White Feathers

Webbed Feet

Natural nibbles

What are the birds at the beach eating? Worms, like the birds in your yard, or maybe something different?

Bird fact

Many birds that live near water have webbed feet. Their feet act like flippers, pushing through the water as they swim.

Tide pool world

There's a world of living creatures to discover in even the smallest tide pool. Grab a net and a bucket and dip in!

To be a star tide pool explorer:

* When dipping your hands in the water, be careful you don't get nibbled!

* Keep creatures in a bucket of water while you take a closer look at them.

* Handle creatures with care and return them to where you found them.

* Always use a net to fish out creatures.

* Don't pull out bits of seaweed—it can take years for it to grow back!

Safety

Stay safe—make sure an adult is keeping an eye out for the tide coming back in.

Dam Building

Have you ever paddled in a stream and felt the pressure of the water as it whooshes past your feet? Well, get ready to stop that water in its tracks!

Start building!

Dams are used to make sure the right amount of water is at the right place at the right time. The dam blocks the flow of the river, so the water builds up behind it to form a large lake, called a reservoir. The reservoir water is used by houses, factories, and farms.

You can find lots of things to build your dam near the stream itself—twigs, branches, rocks, stones, gravel, and mud. The more friends you have to help with the dam building, the better.

Always remember to remove the dam before you go and leave everything as you found it.

YOU WILL NEED

- Large stones
- Smaller stones and gravel
- Mud
- Small branches and twigs

Large stones are essential for a sturdy base.

Criss-crossed twigs, mud and gravel fill any small holes.

Be an engineer

An engineer is someone who designs and builds things—machines, roads, bridges, dams and more—and you can be one, too! While you're building your dam, think about its design and the materials you are using. Which materials hold back the water best? What happens if you change the design? Try using the smaller stones on the bottom and the larger ones on top and see what happens.

Step by step

Hunt for some sturdy stones to make your own stepping stone path across the stream. Secure the stones by digging a base for them in the stream bed, and then pack them in with gravel and pebbles. Make sure they're not wobbly, then start stepping!

Add strips of bark for the finishing touch.

Safety

Never play in water unattended. Ask an adult to help you find a shallow stream that's safe to play in.

Pebble Play

There are tons of cool games you can play on a pebbly beach—you can even practice becoming a super skipper!

Skipping stones

Find a safe place to stand at the edge of a calm sea or lake and have your stones ready. See who can make their stones bounce the most times across the water. Award a shell or pebble for every bounce a player gets. The player with the most bounces wins!

Skip like a pro

Smooth, flat stones the size of the palm of your hand make the best skippers.

Balance the stone on top of your middle finger and use your thumb and forefinger to spin the stone through the air.

Get as low down to the ground as you can and throw straight out, keeping your stone as close to the water as possible.

Before you throw, always check there are no swimmers or birds nearby!

Pebble pics

Start by collecting groups of pebbles that are the same color —dark gray ones, snowy white ones, coral-colored ones. Then use them to create your own seaside creature on the beach!

Bottle bashing

Bury an empty plastic bottle 2 inches deep in the sand. Players take turns throwing pebbles at the bottle until either it falls over—or, if you are timing each turn, the player's time runs out!

Go green

Make sure you take the plastic bottle home with you and recycle it.

Seaside Souvenirs

If you know where to look, the seashore is a trove brimming with treasure! Grab a bucket and go hunting for little gems such as pretty shells, wave-softened glass, shiny seaweed, and colorful starfish.

I see seashells

Big ones, tiny ones, swirly ones—the beach is awash with amazing shells! But did you know that these shells are the homes of small creatures called mollusks? If you find a living creature in one of the shells you collect, be sure to return it to a safe spot, like a rock pool.

Be a rock expert

A geologist is an expert who studies rocks and minerals, which are what sand is made from. To be a geologist yourself, take a close look at some sand. You might see tiny bits of brown or white quartz or pink coral. At home, pour vinegar on your sand. If any of the grains give off tiny bubbles, they were once alive and are actually tiny pieces of coral, bone, or shell!

YOU WILL NEED

- Skewer
- Piece of driftwood
- 8-inch length of string
- Markers
- Selection of small shells and pebbles
- Glue (clear drying)
- An adult helper

Driftwood decoration

Having this cool decoration hanging around will remind you of the fun you had on the beach!

1 Ask an adult to help you skewer a hole in the top of the driftwood. Make a short string loop and knot securely.

2 Draw a simple, striking design on the driftwood. Something seaside-themed would be perfect!

3 Following the marker outline, carefully glue the shells and pebbles in place.

4 Hang up your decoration and enjoy your seaside memories!

Tip

To clean empty shells, soak them in warm water and gently brush with an old, soft toothbrush.

Our Green Street

A team of neighbors working together can transform a street into a lush oasis, bursting with plants and flowers. Here are some ways you can green your own neighborhood…

Window boxes

Check if the window box will be in the sun or shade, and choose colorful plants that are suitable for those conditions. Adding hanging plants—such as tumbling tomatoes and sugar snap peas—will make your window box look, smell, and taste fantastic!

GET PERMISSION

Before you create anything in a public space, even something green and beautiful, you need to have permission from your neighbors, and whoever owns the land. Ask an adult to help you arrange this.

Be a guerrilla gardener

Guerrilla gardeners plant flowers and vegetables on uncared-for spots in towns and cities. You can be a guerrilla gardener by making seedbombs. Throw your seedbombs onto grassy spots that need cheering up. The seeds will grow into flowers that look great—and will also attract wildlife to your neighborhood!

Seedbombing

Seedbombs are easy to make…
and fantastic to launch!

1 Use your hands to mix the clay powder and potting soil in a bowl, then add a teaspoon of seeds and mix.

2 Add small amounts of water to form a paste. Split the paste into six parts.

3 Between flat palms, roll the paste into six balls and place them on a tray covered in tissues.

4 Dry the seedbombs in a warm, dark place (such as a pantry or closet) for 24 hours.

5 Check the weather and if rain is forecast, it's the perfect time to go seedbombing!

Tip Store your dried seedbombs in an airtight container in a dark place until you are ready to launch them.

Street Art

Your street is a blank canvas, waiting to be livened up by eco-friendly art. Transform it using colored chalk, moss, and a lot of imagination… but ask permission first!

Chalk art

Pavement art is easy to create using colored chalk, and washes off when you are done, but don't forget to ask permission before you get creative! Wow your neighbors with your artistic creations, or have fun drawing around your friends' outlines.

Just an illusion…

With a bunch of chalk and a lot of skill, street artists can create amazing 3-D pavement art that looks real enough to fall into or climb up! These talented artists have an amazing ability to trick the eyes of passersby into seeing 3-D images on a completely flat surface. It takes time to create… but the impact is incredible!

Grow your own graffiti

In many urban spaces you'll see colorful graffiti sprayed or stenciled on walls, buildings, and bridges. Moss graffiti is an eco-friendly way of growing art on an outdoor wall. Make sure it's one you have permission to paint!

1 Add the water, yogurt or buttermilk, sugar, and moss to the blender. Blend until smooth.

2 Pour the mixture into a bucket. Chalk a design onto the wall and then color it in using the mixture.

3 Spray with water daily for several weeks and then once weekly to keep your graffiti alive.

Watch your graffiti grow!

Tip If you want to change the design, you can remove your moss graffiti by spraying it with lime juice.

Urban Safari

You don't have to be trekking through the Amazon to see wild and wonderful things. Whether you live in a concrete jungle or leafy suburbia, take a walk on the wild side down the streets of your neighborhood!

Wildlife zone

Choose an area to explore—maybe a few streets around your home. Take a camera, pen, and paper so you can keep a record of what, where, and when you make a find in your wildlife zone. Pay close attention to what's on the ground. If you turn over stones and bits of wood, you may find prehistoric woodlice and other creepy crawlies. Be careful when you put the stone back not to crush any insects.

Urban Safari this way 〉〉〉〉

Safari spot

Make a list of types of urban wildlife to spot, and come up with a scoring system. Easy-to-find animals have lower points and trickier-to-find ones have higher points. Each player has their own list and a pencil. Mark animals off the list when you see them. You can play during the day or at night —just adjust your list to suit the time. Here are some ideas to get you started…

Safari Hit List

Bug life	POINTS
Single insect	5
Insect nest or web	10
Pollinator in action	15

Tweet, tweet	
Seeing a bird	5
Hearing a bird	10
Seeing a bird feeding	15

What am I?	
Small mammal	2
Large mammal	5
Amphibian	10
Reptile	20
Out of the Zone!	50

FOR a spot that's out of its natural habitat, like a cliff-nesting seabird on a city rooftop!

Street Party

Even parties are better outdoors! A street party is a great way to bring your neighborhood together, with yummy things to eat and drink and plenty of fun activities. Let's get the party started!

Getting organized

You'll need to ask your parents to talk to the city council where you live to arrange to close off the street. Once that's been done and the date is set, you can get busy making sure the party goes with a swing...

Decide on a theme

It could be a general theme, like animals, or a theme based on the name of your street, or something your neighborhood is known for.

Make and deliver invitations

Include important information such as the theme, date, and time, and what people should bring.

Make banners and flags

Create a festival atmosphere by recycling old clothes or curtains to make colorful banners and flags.

Tables and chairs

Speak to your neighbors and see who can bring what—garden furniture is ideal for a street party and gazebos are useful, too.

Food and drink

Draw up a list of yummy food and drink you'll need and ask each family to bring something from the list.

Make music

Get together a box of musical instruments—maracas and whistles always help get a party started!

Activity ideas...

There are lots of great activities you can do at your street party to bring everyone together. Here are just a few suggestions to get you started...

Get sporty!

Get your street party off to an energetic start:

* egg-and-spoon races

* sack races

* three-legged races

* tug-of-war

You could also learn some circus skills—see if any of your neighbors can juggle, and ask them to teach you!

Get artsy!

The creative fun doesn't have to stop at making banners:

* colorful chalk murals

* funky face masks

* face painting

* portrait painting

Get thinking...

Write up some questions for a quiz. You could base them around some of these ideas:

* the street's history

* the street's families

* the party theme

* general knowledge

You could assign each family as a team. Don't forget to arrange a prize for the winner!

Why not see how many of the activities and adventures in this book you can incorporate into your street party? Introduce your neighborhood to the Great Outdoors!

Discover More

Look through this selection of websites for more terrific tips, fascinating facts, and incredible inspiration for having outdoor fun!

IN THE YARD

Find out more

Bee facts and identification tips
www.pestworldforkids.org/pest-guide/bees/

Getting wildlife in your garden
www.wildaboutgardens.org.uk/things-to-do.aspx

What else can I do?

Make a cool bird feeder
www.greatgrubclub.com/bird-feeder

Plant a vegetable garden
extension.illinois.edu/firstgarden/

DURING THE NIGHT

Find out more

Sunrise and sunset times worldwide
www.timeanddate.com/

The moon's phases—using cookies!
spaceplace.nasa.gov/oreo-moon/en/

When to see meteor showers
stardate.org/nightsky/meteors

What else can I do?

Identify animals at night
www.kidsplanet.org/games/js/whoami.html

Join international dawn chorus day
www.idcd.info

Play astronomy games and activities
www.kidsastronomy.com

IN THE PARK

Find out more

Photographing wildlife
http://www.bbc.com/earth/world

What else can I do?

Super snail racing
www.thingamababy.com/baby/2007/11/snailrace.html

Raise your own butterfly
www.kidsbutterfly.org/faq/catching/4/

IN THE WOODS

Find out more

What else can I do?

Build a great den
http://www.edenproject.com/learn/for-everyone/
how-to-build-your-own-den/

Make some land art
www.letthechildrenplay.net/2010/08/
land-art-for-kids.html

WINDY DAYS

Find out more

Why the wind blows and other facts!
www.weatherwizkids.com/weather-wind.htm

What else can I do?

Make a simple weather vane
www.sciencekids.co.nz/projects/windvane.html

RAINY DAYS

Find out more

Why it rains and other cool facts!
www.weatherwizkids.com/weather-rain.htm

Measuring rain
easyscienceforkids.com/rain-gauge-experiment-video-for-kids/

What else can I do?

Make a mud pie
www.ntsouthwest.co.uk/2013/07/13-make-a-mud-pie/

SUNNY DAYS

Find out more

How a sundial tells the time
www.liverpoolmuseums.org.uk/kids/games-quizzes/sun/san5.html

What clouds are made of
www.weatherwizkids.com/weather-clouds.htm

What else can I do?

Make a daisy chain
www.wikihow.com/Make-a-Daisy-Chain

Cook some campfire food
www.kids-cooking-activities.com/kids-campfire-cooking.html

NEAR THE WATER

Find out more

Fascinating facts on dams and beavers
www.sciencekids.co.nz/sciencefacts/engineering/dams.html

www.nationalgeographic.com/animals/mammals/b/beaver/

Rocking rock pools—what to look for
www.bbc.co.uk/nature/habitats/Tide_pool

What else can I do?

Play Pooh sticks
www.pooh-sticks.com/content/rules

Make a pond viewer!
https://learning-center.homesciencetools.com/article/pond-life-science-projects/

ON THE STREET

Find out more

Seed ball recipe
https://climatekids.nasa.gov/seed-ball/

Amazing street art
www.mediagang.co.uk/3d-street-art-examples

What else can I do?

Make some online street art
kids.tate.org.uk/games/street-art/

Build a city birdbath
fun.familyeducation.com/activity/birds/39472.html

Index

Credits

The publishers would like to thank the following for permission to reproduce the following photographs in the book:

p16 Shutterstock/Hintau Aliaksei

p23 [T] NASA; [B] Shutterstock/Shalygin

p24–25 Fotolia

p31 [T] Shutterstock/Yellowj; [M] Shutterstock/leungchopan; [B] Shutterstock/Michael G. Mill

p33 Shutterstock/ Alex Staroseltsev; Shutterstock/as3

p35 Shutterstock/ Ivan Smuk

p37 Shutterstock/Eric Broder Van Dyke

p38 Fotolia

p44 Shutterstock/Andrew Chin

p47 Shutterstock/ natuska

p53 Fotolia/Christas Vengel

p63 Shutterstock/Anatoly Kovtun

p70 Shutterstock/hans engbers